ASHOKAN FAREWELL

Fingerstyle Guitar Arrangement

BY JAY UNGAR
ARRANGED BY JOHN LEHMANN-HAUPT

Ashokan Farewell

Arranged by
John Lehmann-Haupt

By Jay Ungar
From the PBS Series
The Civil War

₵II
CV
CII
₵V
CVIII
₵II
CII
₵VII
₵II
₵III
₵II
₵II
CII

₵VII
₵II
CV
XII
IX